PULSING THROUGH MY VEINS

RAW AND REAL STORIES FROM AN ENTREPRENEUR

BLAIR KAPLAN VENABLES

> Hi,
> I will be forever grateful for you + our friendship! You are so special and I love you. Thanks for all of the support. Keep being awesome!!
> ♡ Blair

For my mother, Sharon. I love you.

PRAISE FOR BLAIR KAPLAN VENABLES

"Baby, she was born this way! If you are a business owner - you know. My good friend, Blair Kaplan Venables shares candid and entertaining stories of her business journey by giving you a glimpse into the reality and spirit of the passionate entrepreneur. Read, listen and learn the lessons she teaches. To me, the message is to be unabashedly proud of the path you've chosen."

— Mike Skrypnek, Founder and CEO, www.GrowGetGive.com Coaching, International Speaker and author of the business owners' guide to success, "Entrepreneur Secrets to a Grow Get Give Life."

"When you have that entrepreneurial spirit, it is impossible to ignore. Blair's book is part teaching mixed with the raw stories of what it really takes to follow your journey. The ups and the downs. The successes and the anxieties. Having that same spirit, I felt every word she wrote. A wonderful reminder to those of us who have been in the game a long time, or for those just starting out, that our paths are never quite what we imagined. Thank you for sharing your journey, Blair!"

— Tami Tate, CEO & Event Producer, Social Media Camp, Founder of SMC Club and CEO, 365 Day Media Group, www.socialmediacamp.ca

"This is a must read for anyone with even the smallest urge to go out on their own and step into the world of being an entrepreneur. Whether you are 20, 40, 60 or 80, this book has simple action steps to get you started on your journey, without putting you into overwhelm, or giving you a sense, you'll never be able to "do it all", as other business books can do. Blair's stories and willingness to be vulnerable in sharing her own life experiences, will instead leave you knowing that you CAN take your ideas and message to the world and build the business you want to build…you just have to get started, and this book is a great place to start."

— Melissa Deally, Registered Health Coach at Better Brain Health, www.betterbrainhealth.info

"Blair is an inspiring entrepreneur and she walks her talk! Sharing her candid and real stories about entrepreneurship she brings the humble back to business. Thank you for being a badass and sharing stories of resilience with the world."

— Theresa Lambert, CEO & Transformational Coach of Theresa Lambert Coaching & Consulting Inc. - find out more at
www.theresalambertcoaching.com

Hire Blair

Blair Kaplan Venables is the edutaining speaker that you need at your next event! To book Blair to speak, M.C., lead a workshop, facilitate a panel discussion or give a keynote:

Blair Kaplan Venables
Blair Kaplan Communications Inc.

604-838-4234
blair@blairkaplan.ca
www.blairkaplan.ca

CONTENTS

What Is an Entrepreneur?	xi
1. The Value of Values	1
2. You Were Born to Be Successful	4
3. Define Yourself Don't Defend Yourself	8
4. $hit or Get off the Pot	12
5. Is It Intuition or Is It Gas?	17
6. Time Has Wings	21
7. Be a Honey Badger	25
8. Making It Rain	30
9. Like, Know and Trust	34
10. I Got It from My Mama	38
11. You Take the Good, You Take the Bad	42
12. Nourish Your Brain	48
13. Giving Selflessly	52
14. Protecting Your Flame	55
15. The Year of Abundance	60
16. Flex Your Resilience Muscle	66
17. This Is Only the Beginning	70
Acknowledgments	73
About the Author	77
Hire Blair	79
Notes	81
Notes	83
Notes	85
Notes	87
Notes	89
Notes	91

WHAT IS AN ENTREPRENEUR?

So, you want to be an entrepreneur? Did you wake up one day and decide this? Or has it already been happening for years and you have finally decided to succumb to it?

The ability to be an entrepreneur is in all of us and it can be hard to resist the pull to be one if it's an idea that you have been exploring.

There are many different definitions of "entrepreneur" floating around out there. Merriam-Webster defines an entrepreneur as "one who organizes, manages and assumes the risks of a business or enterprise."

It's true. Being an entrepreneur is risky, but worth it. At the age of 23, at the beginning of the recession in 2008, I left my job to start my company. I was new to living in Vancouver so I didn't have the connections that one should have when starting a public relations company (or any company) – but I felt invincible. I couldn't find an opportunity that I wanted, so I created my own.

This experience, which we visit later on in this book, was part of my journey and an important part of my life. My lessons are shared throughout this compilation of advice so you can hit the ground running and learn from my mistakes.

Being an entrepreneur takes a lot of work, grit, time, commitment and resilience. If you have exposure to entrepreneurs in your life, meet with them and learn about their experiences. If you don't personally know someone and you are thinking about starting a business, try and find a mentor.

Having your own business is an adventure. It can be frustrating and hard while at the same time extremely rewarding. If you have a job and you want to make the transition, start building your company as a side hustle. Alternatively, you can be an entrepreneur within your job by treating your position like a business, which would make you an intrapreneur. An intrapreneur is when someone behaves like an entrepreneur while working within a company that they do not own, which in turn helps to elevate that organization.

Do what you need to do to make your dreams come true. Work before you have to go work, on your lunch break, on the bus/train home from work, after work and on weekends. If you want it bad enough, you will find the time to build your company. If you want it bad enough you will make the time to build your business. I recommend that you wait until you have reached set goals, as well as have a steady income coming in, before taking the leap into full-time business ownership.

If you are reading this book and thinking about starting your own company, if you are deep into your side hustle, if you have just become a full-time entrepreneur or if you have been pounding the pavement for many years, I'm proud of you.

My entrepreneurial friends, this book is for you. I was born an entrepreneur. I will die an entrepreneur. These are just a few of my learnings.

1
THE VALUE OF VALUES

"Your beliefs become your thoughts. Your thoughts become your words. Your words become your actions. Your actions become your habits. Your habits become your values. Your values become your destiny."

- Mahatma Gandhi

THE CONCEPT OF CORE VALUES WAS INTRODUCED TO MY LIFE when I began working for lululemon athletica in 2005. When our Winnipeg cohort began training, we learned their seven core values: quality, product, integrity, balance, entrepreneurship, fun, and greatness. These core values helped guide the company in every decision that they made, including hiring and motivating their employees.

If this is your first time hearing the term "core values", make sure that you take note because they are quite important. Core values are the essential beliefs of a person or organization and they help to guide behaviours. These core values help to steer the moral compass and will act as a guide in decision-making.

It wasn't until I started my own company in 2008 that I began living by my own core values. Over the years those values have evolved. Upon reflecting on the last 11+ years, the one core value that is always front and center is integrity. Having integrity means that I am honest and have strong moral principles to always do what is right. If I work with a client, I need to make sure that they are aligned with this value. I simply cannot work with someone who does not have integrity.

Integrity is my main guiding compass and the nucleus of every project I take on. It inspires the way I conduct business and should be a priority for people who I work for and with. When having core values, you are more likely to be aligned with the essence of your business and your customers.

Another great example of core values were developed by an organization I admire, Zappos:

- Deliver WOW Through Service
- Embrace and Drive Change
- Create Fun and A Little Weirdness
- Be Adventurous, Creative, and Open-Minded
- Pursue Growth and Learning
- Build Open and Honest Relationships With Communication
- Build a Positive Team and Family Spirit
- Do More With Less
- Be Passionate and Determined
- Be Humble

Once you have set your core values, I recommend you share them. You can publish them on your website and/or social media, or print them out and put them up in your office or place of work. You can get creative. Make sure you share them with your entire team, especially when you train someone new.

As I mentioned, my core values have changed over time, but right now I'm driven by the values of integrity, fun, creativity and communication. Those four values help guide my business decisions, how I spend my free time and they led me to be inspired to write this book. Think about what's important to you and use that as a launchpad to set your core values.

Key Takeaways:

1. Create a list of core values to help guide your business growth and decision-making process.

2. Spend time researching the core values of companies you admire, which may inspire you and your values.

3. Like Gandhi says, your values will become your destiny.

2
YOU WERE BORN TO BE SUCCESSFUL

"People who succeed have momentum. The more they succeed, the more they want to succeed, and the more they find a way to succeed. Similarly, when someone is failing, the tendency is to get on a downward spiral that can even become a self-fulfilling prophecy."

- Tony Robbins

SUCCESS MEANS DIFFERENT THINGS TO DIFFERENT PEOPLE. I THINK as a person grows and evolves, their definition of success will always be changing. It doesn't necessarily mean that if you have success, you have money. It doesn't mean that if you're successful, you have happiness. It doesn't mean that if you are successful, you have what you would consider to be a perfect family.

Throughout life there are many different benchmarks and only you, the person in charge of your life, are qualified to set those goals. I guess the definition of success for yourself truly begins with what your goals are.

I have never set a goal to be "successful" because I believe I have a skewed perception of what that actually means. As a child, I deemed success was achieved when you had a big fancy house and a fantastic job title. As I got older, I learned that a lot of those people aren't happy (usually because they end up working all the time and can't enjoy life). And so, my benchmarks of what success means to me are based around personalized milestones and the level of happiness in my life.

I know that as a public relations professional it is a part of my job to manage your perception of me. However, the truth is that imposter syndrome is something I'm constantly battling with. When my businesses first started to grow, I was open about my successes and professional accomplishments. What I learned was that not all of those wins resulted in making my bank account lush. I was featured in a few articles and a book about women business owners, which helped to put my name out there. To the naked eye, I was becoming successful.

Behind the scenes, I was struggling to make ends meet. Financially, I wasn't comfortable and was hardly able to pay my bills. To the outside world, a different story was being told. I was in my early 20's and I not only owned a public relations company, but I had built and created an online health and wellness community.

To many people, this looked impressive. People would reach out to me to discuss my success, but the truth is, I felt like a fraud. In retrospect, I was successful at the time, but I had false expectations about what success meant to me. I was slightly delusional about how much income I should be earning at that stage of entrepreneurship, but the accomplishments that I obtained were what catapulted my future success.

At this point in my life, success is determined by a few factors. I know I'm achieving professional success when I'm doing work that I feel passionate about and when people pay me what I'm worth for that work. I know that I am achieving success when I have to turn down clients because of the workload on my plate. I know that I feel successful when I receive accolades and testimonials from people in my business community, from clients or from friends. I know I'm successful when business referrals land on my desk. I know I'm successful when I'm not lying awake at night stressed about the work I have to accomplish. I know I'm successful when I can take a vacation without worrying about my finances.

WHEN I SET GOALS AND ACHIEVE THEM, I FEEL SUCCESSFUL. EACH goal achieved helps build momentum to achieve my next goal. Like Tony Robbins shared, "the more you succeed, the more you will want to succeed and the more you will feel a sense of success." So, set yourself up to win and to succeed.

I challenge you to create benchmarks that will determine what success means to you. These accomplishments don't need to be large and I suggest that you make them measurable and attainable. The feeling that you are achieving milestones and that you are successful not only helps you to achieve other goals, but helps to motivate you to keep going. Always keep working towards whatever is next on your list of goals, and don't ever quit.

Key Takeaways:

1. Figure out what you need to achieve in order to feel successful and write those goals down.

2. Your definition of success will always change and that is okay.

3. A juicy number in your bank account doesn't always mean you are successful because if you are unhappy and don't have time to enjoy life, is all of that money even worth it?

3
DEFINE YOURSELF DON'T DEFEND YOURSELF

"If you're not branding yourself, you can be sure others do it for you."

- Unknown

DID YOU KNOW THAT YOU ARE YOUR OWN BRAND? YUP, IT'S TRUE. This is something that applies to everyone, especially us entrepreneurs. You see, your business is essentially an extension of you while being a completely different entity (confusing, right?). But you, the owner of the business, will have a reputation to build and maintain.

I've had many clients over the years. Most of them have been great at reputation management and maintaining a professional personal brand. Usually these clients walk their walk and talk their talk. They are usually well-mannered, professional, and polite - customers want to work with them.

. . .

ON THE OTHER HAND, I'VE HAD EX-CLIENTS THAT I DON'T EVEN want to be associated with. One of my clients was rude to suppliers, took advantage of people who wanted to help them and did not pay people they needed to pay (including me). Needless to say, this person put their brand reputation on the line and immediately labelled themselves as someone that people did not want to be associated with. You do not want to be like this person.

Whether you have a job or are self-employed, simply being human means that you have a personal brand. This includes how you dress, how you talk, the words you choose to use, the way you interact with people and everything else under the sun. If you are being your authentic self, you don't need to invent or create your brand, but there are basic things that you can do to maintain it.

IF YOU HAVE A SOCIAL MEDIA PRESENCE, MAKE SURE THAT YOU NOT only fill in all of your profiles, but share and publish content that represents you. If you have a website, make sure to constantly update it. This includes the website's copy, design and functionality.

It's a really good idea to have your business cards on you at all times and hand them out when you meet new people. Do not hand out business cards that are bent, ripped or covered in food. What you wear does matter, to an extent. It's important to try and look professional (whatever that may mean to you), that your clothing is washed and that you don't smell bad.

Always work a room. When I walk into the room of an event, I walk in with confidence and purpose. When I first started my business, my rent was $1300 a month, plus I had bills to pay and debt to clear. I made sure that I never publicly showed signs that my groceries were from the bargain store or that I was making $5 stretch as far as I could. I would never confirm to the world the truth that I was a struggling entrepreneur.

Just to be clear, it is okay to struggle and if you are having trouble financially, it's 100% okay to get a job while you build your business. While growing my company I sometimes had part-time jobs. I would always remain confident, no matter how empty my wallet was.

I made sure I had a few outfits that made me feel smart and powerful. To me, a good blazer paired with earrings and heels transforms me into the business women that you see on television. This combination makes me feel powerful, smart and invincible. I recommend that you find a few wardrobe items and accessories that make you feel the same. You want the worries of life to melt away when you put these items on. When you walk into a room, you will impress people while making a lasting impression.

THE WAY YOU INTRODUCE YOURSELF TO NEW PEOPLE WILL ALSO matter. I suggest memorizing a 30-second elevator pitch that you have ready for when you meet new people. I have a few that I switch between and on the way to an event I rehearse what I'm going to say at least five times in a row. I like to start with my name and business, share a common issue that my services can help solve and then share how I can solve that problem. I also try and spend more time learning about the other people in the room, their businesses and their needs.

You only have one chance to make a first impression and if you take the time to plan out what that first impression will be, you know that people won't forget you. You have the power to be in control of how you present yourself to other people and this lucrative opportunity may open doors that you never even knew existed.

Key Takeaways:

1. Doing laundry and showering are very important things to do. People won't want to meet with you if you don't have good personal hygiene.

2. You have only one chance to make a first impression while telling people what you are all about. Don't blow it.

3. Your elevator pitch is more important than you think. There are many resources online that will help you with a script and by having one of these in your hypothetical back pocket, you will impress a lot of people.

4
$HIT OR GET OFF THE POT

"You miss 100% of the shots you don't take."

- Wayne Gretzky

SOME MAY SAY THAT MY ENTREPRENEURIAL JOURNEY BEGAN WHEN I was a child. I have vague memories of setting up a lemonade stand with my best friend and her sister. We sold juice because we didn't actually have lemonade. If you fast forward to when I was twelve, I proudly became an Avon lady.
You might be thinking "but how? You were just a kid." Well, I wanted to make my own money and be able to purchase my own makeup. So, my mother signed up as an Avon distributor and I went door-to-door selling makeup.

ACCORDING TO MY MOTHER THAT LASTED ABOUT ONE YEAR. I WAS also very excited to become a certified babysitter. Also, at the age of twelve, as soon as I got my babysitting certificate, I began to take on clients. I felt more than ready to eat other people's snacks, watch their children and make some serious coin. I was ambitious and ready to take over the world.

In my late teens, I was lucky enough to be chosen as one of the Educators hired to help open the lululemon athletica store in Winnipeg. I was brought on in 2005 and was blessed with a career in three of their Canadian stores over the next three and a half years.

When employee training began, the world of personal and professional development really opened my eyes and I started on a life-changing journey. Goal setting, which is extremely important to lululemon, and their core value of 'entrepreneurship' are two things that really resonated with me. I felt empowered to be an intrapreneur and to treat my role each day at the store as if it were my own business. If I was in charge of the pants wall that day, I would treat that wall as if I owned it.

If I was the DOFI (Director of First Impression), I greeted everyone as if I were welcoming them to a store that I owned. If you ask anyone who knew me during those days in Winnipeg, there is a good chance they came in and bought clothing from me and could feel my passion.

Upon completion of my Public Relations program at the University of Winnipeg's Division of Continuing Education in 2007, I was promoted within lululemon and moved to the West Edmonton Mall location. I took on the role of Community Leader and I loved it. I had an amazing team and position, however, I learned that Edmonton was not where I wanted to plant roots. So, I made my way to Vancouver in 2008.

I transferred to a Key Leader position at a lululemon location in downtown Vancouver. I had hopes of being promoted to work at their Store Support Center and work with the Public

Relations team. However, it quickly became evident that this was not going to happen.

You see, once upon a time, when the company was privately owned, it seemed easier to move up within the organization. By the time I made it to Vancouver, the company was public and being buffed up with experienced talent from other organizations. My dream of working at their head office became unattainable so I decided to make a career pivot.

It was time for me to shit or get off the pot. At the ripe age of 23, I decided to start a public relations company. To be honest, I had no idea what I was doing. A friend gave me some advice on what to do and I listened to every word, even if some of the advice wasn't correct. I knew I needed a website and business cards and this meant I got to create my own logo. To me, branding myself was one of the most exciting aspects of business ownership. With my branding in place, my website up and my business cards printed, all I needed were clients.

Simultaneously, I was still exploring a new city and checking out all of the copious yoga studio options. My employment at lululemon introduced me to the world of yoga. One of the benefits of working there was that I had access to complimentary yoga and fitness classes.

I was still trying to maintain the lifestyle that I built during my lululemon era, but was now having to pay for these classes out of my pocket. Y'all, I had no idea how expensive yoga was.

BEING THE DAUGHTER AND GRANDDAUGHTER OF COUPONERS, I knew how to look for a coupon resource that would provide me with a way to explore these types of activities at less of a cost. However, my research told me that this resource did not exist. Being the resourceful human that I am, I decided I would start a health and wellness coupon book for Vancouver and call it Living Free Vancouver.

I went to all of the spots that I was curious about, including yoga studios, fitness studios, travel companies, art classes and beyond, and offered them an opportunity to become a part of my project. There was no cost to them and they all agreed to provide me with a coupon for the book. I convinced some of Vancouver's biggest health and wellness companies to help me make my new dream come true.

I decided that I better go out and meet people to spread the word about Living Free Vancouver and my addiction to networking began. I found myself going to multiple networking events a week — morning, noon and night — to spread the word about my coupon book.

OTHER BUSINESS OWNERS EXPRESSED CURIOSITY IN THE COUPON world that I was creating and I would take almost every meeting that was requested of me. Upon learning my story, the conversation would always loop back to public relations, social media marketing and how my services could help their business. Little did I know, the fact that I was able to take an innovative idea (that didn't yet exist in one of the "health meccas" of the world) and make it happen with large organizations proved that I could get shit done. I spoke with conviction and passion. I made things happen. The conversation would always begin with the coupon book and end with how my public relations services could help grow their business.

Over the next few years, my coupon book evolved into a Canada-wide online health and wellness community offering coupons. The format morphed a few different times and the company finally started to grow. But one day I woke up and had an epiphany. I never wanted to own a coupon company. All I wanted was free yoga. This passion project was casting a shadow over the potential of my PR company and sucking a lot of time and energy out of me. With a heavy heart, I decided that

I would no longer be a coupon company business owner and that I was going to focus all of my creative energy on growing my PR business.

I don't think my PR company would have evolved in the fantastic way that it did if it wasn't for my dive into the world of coupons. If it weren't for my mom, who almost always believes in me, I wouldn't be where I am today. If it weren't for Joel Grenz and Motiontide, who helped me build a coupon website while creating custom group buy software, I wouldn't be where I am today. If it weren't for the curiosity and supportiveness of Vancouver business community, I wouldn't be where I am today or who I am today.

I wanted to work in the field of Public Relations and instead of waiting for an opportunity to come knocking, I decided to build my own damn door and walk on through it (while holding a coupon book). I took a shot, just like Wayne said to do.

You are in control of your dreams, and truly, you are the only one who can make them come true. Life is short, so figure out how you want to spend it and make that shit happen.

Key takeaways:

1. Spend time networking in your community. Share with new connections because you never know who may support you and help you grow.

2. Don't own a coupon company. It's a lot of work and in the end, you might as well just pay for the yoga class.

3. Shit or get off the pot. If you want to do something try to figure out how to make that thing happen. Trust me, it's in you.

5
IS IT INTUITION OR IS IT GAS?

"When the universe compels me toward the best path to take, it never leaves me with "maybe," "should I," or even "perhaps." I always know for sure when it's telling me to proceed - because everything inside me rises up to reverberate "YES!"

- Oprah Winfrey

HOW MANY OF YOU HAVE LEARNED TO TRUST YOUR GUT AND follow your instincts? I'm sure that when you were first mastering this skill, you weren't fully aware of that sensation you got when you were about to make a decision that the universe thought was incorrect. My gut has directed me to a lot of fantastic opportunities and delicious desserts, but I've also ignored my gut and got myself into a few terrible situations.

If you don't know what it feels like when your gut is telling you that a situation isn't meant for you, let me explain. Imagine you're faced with a tough decision. Your brain is telling you to do something that makes you feel like your intestines are balled up in the middle of your stomach and you want to gag a little. That's a sign. This is your gut, also known as your intuition, giving you signs to walk away because this experience isn't for you. Your gut can also give you signs that you are on the right path - this feeling is more like butterflies and happy feelings floating around inside of you.

There are a few specific situations that I've got myself into where I know I should've trusted my gut. I often want to see the good in people and believe that the glass is indeed half-full, but it's not always so cut and dry. In the early stages of my career I was looking for guidance and mentorship from more seasoned and successful business owners. On social media I was connected to a very successful businessman who is old enough to be my grandfather. I requested that we meet because I was looking for a mentor. I also thought there was a potential opportunity for this man and I to work together.

We communicated about the potential of me working for him and becoming his assistant. This seemed like a great opportunity to learn from an entrepreneur who had successfully built his own, very large, empire. What he had in mind was something completely different. After our first dinner, at a trendy and popular Vancouver restaurant, I was elated that he presented me the opportunity to work with him. Oddly enough, I was left with a weird feeling in my stomach. I tried to ignore that feeling and focus on the positive and unique opportunity that I was being presented.

AT OUR SECOND DINNER, WHEN I BROUGHT UP MY ROLE WITHIN his organization, he steered the conversation in a very uncomfortable way. He told me that I would be going on business trips with him and that I would be the first person he saw in the morning and the last person he saw before bed. He told me that his wife would not know about me and made some very inappropriate comments that left me feeling gross. The professional relationship that I thought we were building immediately became tainted and dissolved right there.

I will never forget leaving that dinner and standing in the pouring rain, calling my boyfriend (now-husband) and crying. I was upset that the fantasy I had about this career opportunity disappeared. I was upset about the way I was treated as a woman. I felt bad for myself and I knew in that moment I should have trusted my gut. This was an important lesson in my career and it helped me learn how to trust my gut, inner guide and intuition.

According to Psychology Today author Al Pittampalli, "Intuition is a highly sophisticated process. We notice patterns through past experiences, store these patterns and associated information into long-term memory, and then retrieve the information when we see these patterns again in our environment."

MOST OF THE TIME I'M REALLY GOOD AT FOLLOWING MY GUT. IT'S usually to the cupboard to eat something salty and crunchy, however, my impulse control is getting better. Since that evening, I learned that it's imperative to follow your gut when making decisions, but not always to your fridge. There were many times where I've had a feeling best described as a pit in my stomach. This feeling is usually the universe trying to give me a sign to abandon ship. Every single time that I've ignored the voices in my head and the feeling in my stomach, it's come around to bite me in my face. Always, in hindsight, I have known that I should've listened to my gut.

Not all aspects of trusting your gut are bad. Have you ever been presented an opportunity that really resonated with you or that could potentially change your life for the better? Sometimes your intuition knows and your gut tells you that this is the right decision.

You know you are on the right path when you wake up every day with a pep in your step. You know you are following your gut when you are not willing to put your personal goals on the line for what you're working on. Everything that you're doing for your business, as an entrepreneur, should be done with 110% passion, drive, and fire. As soon as any of those three things are compromised, it's time to reflect. If you have that pain in your stomach, that feeling in your throat or that lack of desire, stop what you are doing. If you feel any of these things, I highly recommend that you take a moment to pause and think about what it is that you really want. Maybe it's time for you to make a pivot?

Key Takeaways:

1. If something seems like it may be too good to be true, there's a good chance that it is.

2. Your gut sends signals to your brain for a reason. Trust those signals.

3. If you do learn something the hard way, don't be hard on yourself. You are only human and us humans make mistakes.

6

TIME HAS WINGS

"How did it get so late so soon? It's night before it's afternoon. December is here before it's June. My goodness how the time has flewn. How did it get so late so soon?"

- Dr. Seuss

THERE ARE A FEW THINGS ON THIS PLANET THAT ARE HARD TO live without. In my opinion, two of the most important things that exist are time and money. There are a lot of other important aspects in life like happiness and love, but time is at the top of my list because it's an extremely precious resource that you will never get more of. I'm sure you've noticed that as you get older, time tends to go by much faster. Come January, I usually feel as though July was just the day before. It feels like I was just in Winnipeg at my grandfather's funeral, because ever since his passing, my life has been a whirlwind.

On the way home from his funeral, my husband and I got in a car accident on the Sea to Sky Highway that left me with whiplash and a concussion. Shortly after the accident, with no time to recover, I was doing a massive product launch in Germany which was exciting, but extremely hard with a brain injury.

After getting home from that trip, I began to heal. I finally started to feel like myself again, and then my husband suffered a heart attack and had quadruple bypass surgery. It's important to note that the hospital is three hours from our home so for three weeks I lived out of a suitcase while, my husband, Shayne, was waiting for surgery and recovered in the hospital.

At the time of writing this chapter, his surgery was over three months ago. We are almost at the end of his recovery, but it feels like only yesterday that we were sitting in the ER. In this situation, I'm happy that time went by in the blink of an eye.

THIS CONCEPT OF TIME FLYING BY BENEFITS US WHEN WE WANT IT to go by fast, like when dealing with a crisis or trauma. However, this feeling of time slipping away can add a layer of panic that life is moving too fast and that we may actually run out of time.

There is nothing more valuable than your time. If you take anything away from this chapter, remember this important fact: You will never have more time. You are given a certain amount of time on this planet. You only have a certain amount of time in the day, in the week, in the month, in the year and in your life. Spend your time wisely.

THERE ARE A LOT OF TIME AND ENERGY VAMPIRES OUT THERE. Some of these people have no respect for your time or your expertise. They want your time and knowledge for free, and these people, eventually, will begin to drain you. Sure, it's fine to give out free tips, but when it comes to accepting meeting requests, it's important to understand what the other person's intention is. If you think this will result in a partnership, client or beneficial business relationship, the meeting is worth it. However, if you are unclear about what the goals of the meeting are, ask the other person and follow your gut upon receiving their response.

People often want to meet with me to share their ideas and try to extract information. Often the meeting request is accompanied by the statement of "I want to pick your brain." Let's think about that for a second. To me, this seems painful. This usually brings up a visualization of two tiny doll sized monkeys sitting on my skull, with the top of my head flipped open, while they pick my brain with dental scalers. Gross, right?

I have far too many experiences with people who want access to my creative insights and knowledge that I've spent many years learning. I am someone who will assess each person's meeting request on an individual basis and if it's a conversation that can be had over the phone, I steer our meeting in that direction. I usually do give out a few tidbits and ideas, but I am strategic about those deliveries.

DON'T GET ME WRONG, NOT EVERYONE WANTS TO MEET TO GET free information. There are people out there who want to meet because they want to work together, share opportunities, or simply want to get to know you better. There are also people out there who know that your time is valuable and will offer to pay you for a meeting or at least take you for lunch or coffee.

Those people who realize how valuable my time is are people that I want to do business with. Those people who respect my time and worth are people who I admire and respect.

Other things that I do to protect my time include working when I know I'm the most efficient. I'm often up at a very early hour so that I can get some work done before emails, calls, texts and social media notifications begin to flow in. I try and work on more of my monotonous tasks or schedule meetings and breaks during my least productive times of the day. If a conversation can be had over the phone or email, I'd rather do that than meet in person — often commuting time can turn a one-hour meeting into a two-hour meeting.

Dr. Seuss understood that importance of time and that time easily disappears. His quote is extremely relatable. Everyone has time and it's best to use it efficiently and treat it as a very precious commodity.

Key Takeaways:

1. Time is one of the most precious resources that you have and our time has a value associated with it.

2. You will never be given more time.

3. Can we all stop asking people if we can pick one another's brains? Yuck! If you want to have a meeting with someone so that you can learn new information, please offer them compensation along with the request to meet.

7

BE A HONEY BADGER

"All progress begins with a brave decision."

- Marie Forleo

According to various resources online, along with the Guinness Book of World Records, the honey badger is considered "the most fearless animal" on Earth. They are known to go after and attack animals who are much bigger than them. The honey badger even has a gland at the base of its tail that stores a stinky liquid and if it is frightened or threatened, it will deploy a horrendous smell.

Different animals show fear in different ways. When a dog is scared it may cower, lick its lips, avoid eye contact or scratch itself. When a cat is scared it may run away and hide, freeze in place or lose control of its bladder. Some bears may run away if they are scared. When ostriches are scared they flop to the ground. Weird facts, right?

    We humans, us complicated beings, have no consistency in our behavior, especially when it comes to reacting to fear. Fear is a feeling that people try to push down and hide, causing it to emerge in weird and unusual ways. In my early 20's I dated men who were wrong for me. Don't get me wrong, a few of my ex-boyfriends are great men, but there are some that stand out as horrible people. I admittedly moved too fast with a particular ex-boyfriend. This resulted in me living with him before I got to know him as much as I should have. After moving in with him I discovered his kryptonite — I learned that he was an alcoholic.

MY SUSPICIONS PROVED TRUE WHEN I STARTED TO FIND EMPTY bottles of alcohol hidden around the home. This was scary for me. I knew I had to leave him and move out, but, at the time, it didn't seem that straightforward.

    For months I was verbally abused when he was highly intoxicated. It would happen when I least expected it. I'm not talking about him just raising his voice and yelling at me. If I came home and he was passed out, I would try to not wake him. I would try to go to sleep, but I would be on edge and pray that the morning would arrive soon. There were a few times that I would wake up to him standing over me while yelling profanities and calling me names that I didn't deserve to be called. It was horrible.

    There was a monumental incident that occurred one spring night and it changed the course of my life. He picked me up at work and it wasn't until we were on the road that I learned he was not sober or safe to drive. He was blackout drunk and I was stuck, in his vehicle, as a very scared passenger. That evening things escalated and he put his hands on me and gripped my neck. That moment shook me to my core and that was the night I left him. I was scared and I didn't know what I was going to do. I spent the night at a coworker's house and the next day I packed my bags and left. This was the rock bottom I needed to hit in order for me to make a massive change in life. I was almost free.

Due to my situation during that relationship, I was in a depression that rendered me unable to work or bring in enough income to make a move on my own. Once this final straw happened, my adrenaline kicked in and my fight or flight switch turned on.

I felt like I finally had courage again so I connected with a few business owners who expressed interest in working together. I did what any resourceful and savvy business woman would do — I called each of them to let them know that there was a limited time offer to work with me and if they wanted to move forward, they had to pay a deposit. These few companies agreed, I picked up my deposits, and I proceeded to secure my own apartment. My next obstacle was to find somewhere to stay for three weeks until I got possession of my new apartment.

DUE TO THE COMBINATION OF A LACK OF FINANCIAL SUPPORT AND not wanting to be a burden on my friends or family, I kept the severity of my situation on the down low. You guys, I *should've* asked for help. If this story is similar to one that you are living, please ask for help. I don't think I really understood the harshness of the situation while I was in it. I was acting fearless because it's what I had to do in order to survive.

At the time, I had a part-time job bartending and one of my colleagues offered me a place to stay where he was housesitting. Every night he would let me in and I would sleep on the couch and every morning I would leave and head back to my former home to shower and get a change of clothes while my ex went to work. I was homeless. This was scary and hard to admit.

I felt like I'd dug my own grave and did it to myself. I felt like I created this reality and it was my job to pull myself out. I had a few friends offer their couches here and there and I definitely took them up on that. Being around familiar faces helped me heal. The day that I moved into my own safe space, I felt liberated. I finally felt a sense of relief, my fear melted away and I was finally able to start a new chapter of my life.

Because of my fearlessness and my ability to figure out how to survive, my business began to thrive. Those new clients launched my business to a new level and I'm not sure if that would have happened if I had stayed with my ex.

It was sink or swim and I chose to swim so fast that I was flying. I felt like I could accomplish anything and I knew that if I set my intentions to achieve a goal, I was going to make it happen. My fear fueled my ambition and my ambition opened doors and made money flow in.

At this stage of life, my fear manifests as anxiety and I feel it every day. I've survived multiple traumas and I'm always working on managing my anxiety; it's a constant struggle.

For example, a current worry of mine is that I won't have the rough draft of this book completed on time, which is silly because these are deadlines that I set. So, until I'm finished this draft, I'm waking up at an ungodly hour so that I can work on this book.

As a matter of fact, I'm currently working out while I type this. I say "working out", but I'm on a bike where you just lean back, chill and pedal. This is the only cardio machine

where I can sweat and type without dropping my phone. I thought about bringing my laptop but then I'd be that weirdo at the gym. I also thought about dictating this chapter, but then the nine other people here would learn one of my secret productivity hacks and still think I'm a loser for being on the phone at 6am at the gym. Really, I should have stayed home to write but I need to work out to help me manage my anxiety.

I'm a "you do what you gotta do" kind of girl. My survival instinct, when it comes to fear, is to put on a brave face and tackle my challenges head on. I learned to do this at an early age and I always look fear in the eyes to conquer it. Take on life like a honey badger and know that no matter what your challenges are, you got this!

Key Takeaways:

1. If you are in an abusive relationship, do what you need to do to get out of it. You don't deserve to be treated that way and there are many people and organizations that can help you leave that relationship.

2. Always do what you have to do to navigate a challenging time.

3. It's okay to be scared and you don't always have to be fearless. You are a human, after all.

8
MAKING IT RAIN

"You can only become truly accomplished at something you love. Don't make money your goal. Instead, pursue the things you love doing, and then do them so well that people can't take their eyes off you."

- Maya Angelou

MONEY CAN MAKE THE WORLD GO AROUND. MONEY CAN ALSO BE at the root of evil. Money is needed to keep a roof over your head, food on your table, the lights on and for the clothes on your back. When I'm driven by passion, the money always ends up making an appearance. I've always been driven by desire first and money second (or maybe third). If I don't love what I'm doing it will impact my ability to be successful and to make a living. However, money is important because we need it to survive.

When I first began my company I was young, naive and thought that collecting payment from clients would be an easy task. Perhaps people felt like they could take advantage of me or perhaps some people are evil — my initial thought was proven to be incorrect and I learned the hard way that not everyone operates with integrity. Most of my clients pay me for my work and pay me on time, but there are a few that did not pay me and I will never forget them.

The few clients that didn't pay me are ones that really changed the way I see business transactions. A specific one that stands out was when I was doing business with a man we will call "Dolphin."

You see, Dolphin had a massive vision to build a company and I was going to do it with him, as his main team member. The business involved yachts, a system to collect points and a potential television show. He also had investors, his own money and affluent people supporting him, so he told me. It almost seemed too good to be true and I should have listened to my gut.

WHEN I BEGAN WORKING FOR DOLPHIN, I WAS RECEIVING consistent pay cheques, but over time I was getting paid late and eventually the lies and stories began to surface. Sure enough, I was stiffed out of lot of money and even though my relentlessness was able to squeeze him for a few more of my hard earned dollars, he eventually disappeared. This was a very bizarre period in my life.

But after working with Dolphin and helping him build a company that never launched and him vanishing before settling his debts, I was inspired to change my business practices. Luckily, I always make sure that I have multiple projects on the go so that there are multiple streams of revenue.

AFTER WORKING WITH DOLPHIN THERE WAS A TIPPING POINT IN

my business and prospective clients were now finding and approaching me. This was nice because it meant that I created a demand for my services. I felt like I was in a good enough position in the market to adjust my payment terms.

To avoid being taken advantage of again, I made a shift into accepting payments via installment plans and would not begin work until the first payment or a deposit was made. I also started to request postdated cheques when contracts would begin (does that make me sound like a dinosaur? Perhaps I'm a Blairasauras?). This ensured that I always had payment and a payment on time.

I'VE SINCE GROWN TO UNDERSTAND THAT EVERY CLIENT IS different. It's really quite unfortunate when payments for delivered work don't happen. I mostly feel bad because, to me, it's a sign that the other business person is struggling.

If an honest conversation is had with me, I'm flexible about payment terms. I've been in situations where I have to break out payments into installments and people who I did business with were kind to me.Besides actually getting paid, which is a pretty big deal, I believe it's important to know your worth. I've noticed that a lot of really smart entrepreneurs don't know their value and are undercharging for their products or services. I truly believe that you will attract the clients you want by not only being really great at what you do, but by taking your experience and time into consideration when setting your rates.

If you have been working for many years in your industry, have a great track record, and have integrity paired with an abundance of expertise, don't sell yourself short. You are worth every penny you charge and your knowledge and contributions are valuable. You deserve to make it rain on yourself.

Key Takeaways:

1. If your industry allows it, create a payment structure that allow you to be paid over the duration of a project and always take a deposit. You can also get post-dated cheques or set up auto charging on a credit card.

2. Decide what you are worth and set your rates to reflect your value and expertise.

3. If someone doesn't pay you, don't give up. Keep knocking at their door, involve a lawyer and make sure that your business community knows about their business misconduct so no one else falls victim to them.

9
LIKE, KNOW AND TRUST

"Your network is your net worth."

- Porter Gale

I WISH I HAD A BETTER MEMORY BECAUSE IF I DID, I WOULD remember who told me some of the most important words I've ever been told. The following words resonated so hard with me that they influence and impact everything I do in building relationships. To me, this is one of the most important lessons that I'm going to teach, so pay attention: People do business with people they like, know, and trust. I know it's a mega cliché but it's fricken' true.

Let me repeat that: People do business with people they like, know, and trust. Now it's your turn. Say it out LOUD: PEOPLE DO BUSINESS WITH PEOPLE THEY LIKE, KNOW AND TRUST.

There are many different ways to build relationships. You obviously want to make a good impression with people you are meeting for the first time but you also want to grow and nurture relationships with people you already know. Networking isn't just meant to be applied to your business life and it's actually something that you should do quite regularly.

As someone whose adrenaline gets pumping when meeting new people, when I briefly took the reins as President for the Whistler chapter of Business Networking International (BNI), I felt like I had accomplished a cool networking milestone. It was as if I had been training for a decade to climb Mount Kilimanjaro and I was finally climbing it, *and* had it made to the summit.

OUR BNI NETWORKING GROUP MET EVERY THURSDAY MORNING AT 6:45am in Whistler, about a half an hour from my home. Business professionals from the area would come to share what they did and the type of business they were looking for. Everyone there had a goal to grow their business.

Upon joining this networking group as a member, my business immediately grew and the return on my initial investment to join was quite evident. Each week I was meeting new business people in the community, I got the stage for at least 45 seconds to advertise my business and I was practicing my public speaking skills.

When the opportunity to be President and run the weekly meetings was presented to me, I was excited to accept the position. I was at the front of the room, managed the meeting, was given more time to speak and was able to bring a Blair-esque energy to the group. I was honoured and very proud of myself because I had big boots to fill.

My reign only lasted six months because a project I was working on took me on the road for an extended period of time. Part of your membership commitment to BNI is that you have to attend each meeting or find a substitute if you cannot attend.

This wouldn't fly if I were gone for more than a few meetings since my position was to run the meeting, this was even more of a challenge. It broke my heart, but I had to step down as President and leave the organization. Staying would comprise my integrity as a leader. It's what I had to do at the time and I can tell you that I miss those weekly meetings.

The concept of networking is quite simple. Networking is when you interact with others and share information, which in turn develops into relationships. Perhaps you were looking for a strategic partner in business? Maybe you are looking for someone to build your website? Your husband flushed something weird down the toilet and you need a trustworthy plumber that will show up, right?

From networking and being out and about there's a good chance that you will come across people who can help you in various aspects of your life.

I'M GENERALLY SOMEONE WHO IS QUITE INCLUSIVE AND I LOVE meeting new people. There's a good chance that when I meet you for the first time I'll let you know that we should be friends and proceed to make plans to hang out with you. I generally see the good in everyone, which is a blessing and a curse.

When it comes to meeting new people in business, something I learned early on was that I loved going to events. I saw this as the golden mecca for networking. The adrenaline that pumped through my veins when I got to introduce myself to multiple people in the short span of a few hours led to a rush that influenced me to function at my highest capacity.

I found networking groups that met early in the morning before most people are out of bed. I discovered lunchtime networking events. I loved the cocktail hour networking events — people would meet after work and eat little hors d'oeuvres that were being passed around. Often, I would station myself beside the door where the servers would emerge. Usually I met a couple of other people who had the same plan of attack: meet cool people while being first to eat the food. I could not get enough of networking. I still can't get enough of networking.

Luckily, I am quite personable and it's easy for me to connect with people because I usually try to find something that I have in common with them. Also, when I meet new people I just want to learn all about them — figure out who they are, what their goals are, and how I can I help them.

Shortly after I left BNI, the Whistler chapter closed. The core members of that chapter created a new group that meets once a month. I go to every meeting that I can and we still meet while most people sleep, early in the morning. I also try and attend at least three other networking or educational events a month and do what I can to network online.

Without networking I would not be where I am today. I owe a lot of my growth to Living Free Canada and the hustle that I had in my early 20s.

Key Takeaways:

1. No matter what stage you are in your business or career, always make the time to be out and about in the business community to build your professional network.

2. If you live somewhere where there is a BNI chapter, I recommend you check it out. Joining BNI helped my business grow and developed me as a business professional.

3. If you are hungry and you want to meet new people while at an event where appetizers will be served, stand near the kitchen. You will be the first to eat and you will meet other people who think like you.

10
I GOT IT FROM MY MAMA

"Family is not an important thing,
it's everything."

- Michael J. Fox

THE BANK OF SHARON OPENED FOR BUSINESS BECAUSE MY mother, Sharon, believes in me more than anyone else in the entire planet. Maybe it's because I throw myself into every passion-fueled project or maybe it's because she's my mom and it's her job to believe in me. Regardless, she is my number one fan and support — no one believes in me more than my mother and she provided the capital to build my coupon company.

As a matter of fact, she was my source for funding when I was twelve years old and started my Avon side-hustle. It was she who fronted me the *cashola* for my business when I started my entrepreneurial journey and it was she who launched me into the world of tech.

Earlier on in this book I shared that I created a coupon company. I couldn't have done that without my mother or The Bank of Sharon. She believed in me and gave me capital to make that company happen. She helped me make that coupon community come to life and that community was an important part of my career.

I'll forever be grateful for all of the businesses who took a chance to work with me in the world of coupons and for my mom, who had complete faith in me and my ability to build a coupon empire. My mother was the reason that I was able to innovate and create a coupon company. Her love for coupons and her believing in me is what powered by business.

There's an important lesson in this story. You see, I was raised primarily by a single mom with the support of grandparents, aunts and uncles and a very loving community. Not once in my life did I feel like I couldn't achieve something. In fact, if there was an opinion that I shouldn't do something, I was more driven to prove that person wrong. I'm stubborn and it's hard for me to let someone else tell me what to do. What I know for sure is that if there is something that I want to do and if I cannot stop thinking about it and I will not stop thinking about it - I will do anything in my power to make sure that I make that thing happen.

I DID A LOT OF TRAVELING WHEN I WAS YOUNGER. WHILE I WAS IN university, I would usually work two jobs so that I could afford my car, have money for a social life, pay off debt obtained from adventures the previous year and allow me to get me started on my next adventures. I worked various retail jobs and, once I was old enough, I worked in the nightclubs selling roses. Believe it or not, selling roses was a great way for me to make extra cash and this job got me into the back door of most of the Winnipeg nightclubs and lounges.

Before my final year at university, I spent the summer living in Greece. Luckily, this was before smart phones and predated the popularity of Facebook. To email home, I went to an Internet Café. To call home, I used a calling card with far too many numbers that I managed to memorize.

That summer was spent on the islands of Corfu and Ios, in Greece. My friend and I started off working at The Pink Palace on Corfu and I was a daytime bartender. After about a month, we decided to move to Ios and see what opportunities lured us in.

SHORTLY AFTER ARRIVING I LANDED A GIG AS A SERVER AT A HEAVY metal rock club. My job was to clean up dishes, take drink orders, do shots with clients and clean the tables and floors (while heavily intoxicated). Being born with the husky 1-900 voice that I have, I am very susceptible to losing my voice, which happened shortly after I took this job. Trying to talk over the loud music along with the constant flow of alcohol was not putting me on the fast track to optimal health.

I couldn't get better, so I decided to quit. I had a juicy limit on my credit card and thought, "Hey, I may as well live it up and pay it all back when I get home." I guess you can say that I'm an expert at living in the moment.

When I arrived back in Winnipeg, I had a plan to pay off my credit card, but I ended up moving across the country, twice, and spent a lot of money that I didn't have. I had a plan set up on how I was going to pay off my debt, but I wasn't able to.

Shamefully, my mother had to bail me out. How selfish am I? My single mother, who put me and my sister through private school and university, sent us to various lessons and to summer camp, had to bail out her grown-ass daughter. The Bank of Sharon didn't want me to have bad credit nor did she charge interest. After this incident, The Bank of Sharon closed.

When Living Free Canada's concept came to life, I didn't ask for capital. My mom saw my passion and fire and offered to help. If I needed to, I would have asked for funding from my family members who believed in me. When I'm fueled by passion, I speak with captivating conviction. Sometimes we all need a little help to get going and if it weren't for the support of my mom, I'm not sure if I would be where I am today or who I am today. I hope that one day I can open the Bank of Blair for my mom and treat her to something really nice. My family is everything to me and I owe a lot to my mother.

Key Takeaways:

1. If you require funding for a business idea, start by sharing your vision with your friends and family

2. Living in Greece is worth every penny that you will spend.

3. We don't give enough credit to single parents so let's all show those single parents in our lives some extra love.

11
YOU TAKE THE GOOD, YOU TAKE THE BAD

"DNA is like a computer program but far, far more advanced than any software ever created."

- Bill Gates

Wise words that resonated with me early into my business ownership journey were "Businesses don't fail, entrepreneurs fail". I wish I remember where I first heard it, but nonetheless, it has stuck with me. In business, I always knew when it was time to make a pivot, push forward or quit. If I were to quit, I would try and quit while I was ahead and on my own terms.

After spending over a decade growing my public relations company, Blair Kaplan Communication Inc., I'm now able to teach and guide new entrepreneurs and inspire them to persevere. I don't think everyone is cut out for business ownership and if you are venturing into our world, be ready to make many sacrifices to drive your business to succeed.

I'm lucky because I've been surrounded by entrepreneurs my entire life. Entrepreneurship is part of my genetic makeup. It pulses through my veins and stokes my passion and fire. I come from a long line of entrepreneurs and in order to help you understand my linage, I'm going to share with you my family tree.

BELLA FISHER

MY FATHER'S GRANDMOTHER, BABA BELLA, WAS A TRUE SHERO. From approximately 1934 to 1974 she owned Belle's Fashion Shop in Winnipeg's Osborne Village.

Yes, that's right folks. A WOMAN owned her own business and was the primary bread winner for her family "back in the day."

Can you say girl power? According to my Baba Leah, her daughter, she was full of piss and vinegar and apparently, I'm a lot like her.

Sadly, I never had a chance to meet her but the stories I've been told lead me to think that we have a lot in common. Not only in namesake, but that part of her soul is rooted deep within mine.

It's a Jewish tradition to be named after a deceased family member and on the Kaplan side of my family, I was the first grandchild to be born. I was given the Hebrew name Baila Deena after my dad's grandmother, Baba Bella, and my mom's grandmother, Aunt Dora.

The English name given to me was Blair Dana. Originally, I was going to have the first name of Brooke but nearing the end of my mother's pregnancy she was inspired by the Facts of Life character, Blair.

She was tall. She was rich. She was blond. She and I were to have the same name. Note to you readers out there, I'm a short, mighty, and curvaceous brunette.

HOOKEY SLAYEN

ZAIDA HOOKEY, MY MOTHER'S FATHER, WAS A MAN I WISH I HAD A chance to get to know. At one point, if you ordered French fries at any food establishment in Winnipeg, there was a good chance those potatoes came from Fruta, Zaida Hookey's fruit and vegetable wholesale business.

Sadly, I was merely a year old when my grandfather passed away, but his legacy lived on for many years after his departure from this earth. My Auntie Heather took over running the business and I spent many years visiting her there. I feel that a slice of my drive comes from him.

SUSAN RYKISS

MY DAD'S YOUNGER SISTER, SUSAN RYKISS, HAS BEEN A VERY important part of my life. Not only was she a very dedicated aunt but she also took me under her wing and show me the entrepreneurial ropes of her newspaper, Winnipeg Parent Newsmagazine.

My sister and I spent a lot of time with Susan and her family. Susan launched her family newspaper in September 1993 and from an early age I was invited to write for her. My first article was about the benefits of sending children to summer camp. Susan also hired me to help with her annual Family Fun and Learning Fair.

This experience was the icing on the cake that directed me

to the Public Relations and Management program at the University of Winnipeg's Division of Continuing Education. Auntie Susan is another true *shero* and I'm lucky to have grown up in the presence of such a kind, driven soul.

I believe that she's a big influence in where I am today in my career.

STUART SLAYEN

My mom's younger brother, Stuart Slayen, has been a mentor and guide since I was a young girl. When I was in elementary school my passion for writing emerged. Uncle Stu was the Editor of KidsWorld Magazine and was kind enough to publish one of my pieces.

In 2009, after nine years as the Publishing/Communications Manager at the International Institute for Sustainable Development, he started his own consultancy. As my business grew, I knew I could go to him for advice. Not only is he full of valuable information, but our time together is usually full of laughs because his humour is like no other. I'm honoured to share genetics with Uncle Stu.

LEONARD KAPLAN

My father wasn't around much in my formative years, but upon reconnecting with him in my twenties, I learned a lot about his life. He was in business with Zaida Hookey. Most interestingly, he's a Certified Graduate Gemologist and was also a diamond dealer.

In the 80's he used computer software to appraise jewelry

and had many affluent, important clients. If you open the Google and care to dive into a vortex, the 1984 and 1985 Stanley Cup rings have some diamonds that Wayne Gretzky purchased from my father. This isn't an opportunity to name drop, this is my opportunity to show you the cool shit that my dad did. Sadly, my dad became unwell, sold the business and is no longer practicing. However, knowing that I have his entrepreneurial skills and passion is pretty special.

SHARON KAPLAN

MY MOTHER, WHO HAS BEEN A DENTAL HYGIENIST FOR 40 YEARS isn't an entrepreneur, but is one of the hardest working people that I know. She worked very hard to give my sister, Alana, and me a good education and life. Being surrounded by her tenacity was inspiring and I know that her work ethic has rubbed off on me.

Other businesses that family members of mine have started and/or owned have been a chocolate factory, hospitals, regional newspapers and media platforms. I believe that my genetics have helped to give me the drive and light the fire in my entrepreneurial soul.

Over the duration of my career I've either been an entrepreneur, an intrapreneur or both at the same time. There have been times when I've had to have a job to help fund my business. There have been times when my capacity was capped and I've had to release clients or rearrange my company's plate. I'm lucky to have the support and guidance of family members who have been on their own entrepreneurial journeys.

With the support and knowledge from my family, I know and understand the failure isn't possible. All I have to do is keep trying and to find what works. If you are reading this and there aren't any entrepreneurs in your life and you want to dive into this world, let me help guide you. Let me be the entrepreneur who helps to inspire you. You got this, so go get 'em, tiger.

Key Takeaways:

1. If you have any business owners in your family, spend time with them to learn more about why they love being an entrepreneur. Ask them questions about their struggles and success while drinking in their knowledge.

2. Businesses don't fail, entrepreneurs fail. If something doesn't work, keep trying to find a solution. Keeping working hard to make it work.

3. If you feel that entrepreneurialism is pulsing through your veins, I encourage you to explore that feeling and deploy that superpower.

12

NOURISH YOUR BRAIN

"Having power is not nearly as important as what you choose to do with it."

- Roald Dahl

SLEEP IS EXTREMELY IMPORTANT. YOUR BRAIN REQUIRES SLEEP IN order to function correctly, and is very important for proper memory function.

According to Brandon Brock, MSN, BSN, DNP, certified family nurse practitioner and staff clinician at the Foundation Physicians Group, "Sleep deprivation kills brain cells, can create psychosis if long enough, and will reduce the ability of the body and the brain to heal." All of the things Brock shared can impact your thought process, awareness, decision-making, and reaction time.

When I started to write this chapter, I was emerging from a Buckley's-nighttime-pill-induced coma; I realized that my goal for being productive on my flight from Vancouver to

Munich had failed. I had the ambition to spend at least a few hours of the flight writing, but that was not the case. I watched the new Aladdin movie and spent the next six hours in and out of bizarre, yet fascinating, dreams. That is what I love about cold medicine to help you sleep - the dreams that transpire.

Sleep is usually a priority for me. It's a time to rejuvenate, recharge and rest. During the fall of 2019, I struggled to recognize myself and wasn't sure of who I was anymore. On the outside, I looked like me, but on the inside, I felt like a zombie with no feelings and no brain. I felt like I was no longer living and I was only existing.

In the middle of summer that year, I was in a car accident. We were in Winnipeg for my grandfather's funeral, which was devastating of its own accord. After an emotionally exhausting trip, my husband and I were finally on the way home from the airport. The drive from the airport to home is a few hours along the Sea to Sky Highways. All that I wanted to do was get home to my own bed and snuggle with my cats. Ten days away from my Pemberton life was too long.

I can't help but fall asleep when I'm the passenger in a vehicle, bus or train. This time, I was the passenger of a truck and while napping is when the accident happened. Upon impact I received whiplash and a concussion. A prefrontal cortex concussion is no joke. For someone like me, who puts food on the table because she's good with ideas, wit, words and juggling multiple projects, this was scary. A brain injury to me is like a soccer player breaking his leg. *No buneo.*

I no longer felt like myself. I felt like the wick of my candle had dwindled down to a tiny nub drenched in wax and was about to go out. Was this the end of me and all of my great ideas?

The prefrontal cortex is at the front of the brain and the frontal lobe is responsible for personal characteristics and our behaviour. This includes personality, voluntary movements, impulse control, problem-solving, motivation, and sexual and social behaviors. When this part of the brain is injured, all of these elements have the potential to be affected.

This injury increased my anxiety and sadness. I found it really hard to be happy. I noticed a big difference in my problem-solving ability and it took me longer to come up with creative ideas. I knew that it would possibly take a few months before I felt like myself again so I began to seek treatment to help me heal.

WHAT I LEARNED THROUGH THIS HEALING JOURNEY IS TO GIVE AN injury time to heal and rest as much as I could. A huge aspect of resting was limiting my screen time, which, as you can imagine, was difficulty for me due to my profession.

Even today, months later, I keep up my healing routine. I continuously feed my brain the information that it needs in order for it to recover. I also know what I need to do to make sure that its function is optimized. I read and listen to audiobooks and podcasts. I go to workshops and conferences and am always working on personal and professional development. I am continuously working on expanding my knowledge and feeding my brain information that will help it thrive.

I also make sure that I get at least seven to eight hours of sleep a night, eat foods that are healthy my brain, and make physical activity a priority. Adrenaline and endorphins help my brain flourish and trigger new ideas to emerge. Rest helps me recharge and gives me power.

Without my brain being what it is, I don't think I'd have the goal or drive to write this book. My career depends on my brain, my skills and most importantly, my creativity. My ideas are what makes me unique and that is why people want to work with me. I owe a lot of thanks to the many people in my community who helped guide me to heal from my concussion. They offered tips about what type of vitamins to take, food to eat and practitioners to see. It took me a few months before I felt like myself again and I'm proud of my brain for bouncing back. If you love your brain, your brain will love you back. I promise.

Key Takeaways:

1. Make rest and sleep a priority.

2. Your brain is one of your most important parts of your body, so take care of it and constantly feed it new information.

3. If you ever have a head injury, take time off to heal. Make sure you seek medical attention and do what you need to do to get your brain back to 100%.

13

GIVING SELFLESSLY

"Never doubt that a small group of thoughtful, committed citizens can change the world; indeed, it's the only thing that ever has."

- Margaret Mead

I STARTED MY VOLUNTEERING JOURNEY AT AN EARLY AGE. LIKE ALL good Jewish tweens, I was scheduled to be Bat Mitzvahed at the pubescent age of 12.

For those of you who aren't aware, I'll give you a quick little lesson. In the Jewish religion, when a boy reaches the age of 13 he is called to become Bar Mitzvah. Because girls become women earlier in life, they are called to be Bat Mitzvah at the age of 12. So, for many months leading up to your debut as a Jewish woman, you begin your training. This training includes learning how to chant from the Old Testament (also known as the Torah), learning and practicing prayers, memorizing a specific portion of the Torah, and attending meetings with the Rabbi, where I learned how to be a better person.

ONE OF THE VALUES THAT WAS INSTALLED IN ME, SOMETHING THAT I still carry with me today, is the concept of volunteering and giving back. During the time leading up to my Bat Mitzvah I decided that I was going to dedicate my volunteer hours to hanging out with seniors who had Advance Alzheimer's.

It felt good to go and hang out with seniors who didn't have many visitors, but when I would greet them, their faces would light up when they saw me. More often than not, I would have the same conversations every visit, but that didn't matter. I knew I was giving back and I knew I was making that moment in their day brighter, even if they weren't going to remember it.

Since those first volunteer days I've done what I can to give back. I've been on multiple fundraising event committees for Ovarian Cancer Canada's British Columbia and Yukon Region; I was a part of the Pemberton Refugee Resettlement Group and helped to raise funds to bring a refugee family to Pemberton, B.C., plus help support them once they arrived; and, at the time of writing this, I'm on the Board of Directors for the Pemberton Chamber of Commerce.

When I donate my time and services, it's often because I feel like I have something to offer to help enhance that organization. Also, when giving my time and expertise, it's usually because that group or organization's purpose resonates with me.

BUSINESS KARMA HAS HAD A BEAUTIFUL WAY OF REWARDING ME, especially because when I volunteer, that desire isn't driven by the need to grow my business. While I was on one committee, another committee member hired me to launch their global ski and golf clothing brands on social media. Another member of that committee hired me to help with social media marketing for their boutique. I was able to display my skills for the team and it piqued the curiosity of others about how I could help them.

The main reason I give back and volunteer is because it feels good to help others. A small action on my behalf can have a huge impact on someone else's life. Since I've been on the volunteer circuit for over two decades, I've noticed that the saying 'what goes around, comes around', shows up in the best possible ways when volunteering.

Key Takeaways:

1. The world needs more volunteers and by donating your time, you could help change the lives of many. Look at your schedule and figure out how you want to give back and make it happen.

2. The universe works in mysterious ways and when you volunteer and give back, you fill up your good-karma bank.

3. Doing good = feeling good.

14

PROTECTING YOUR FLAME

"If you take care of your mind,
you take care of the world."

- Arianna Huffington

BURNOUT IS SOMETHING THAT I WOULDN'T WISH UPON MY WORST enemy. It's something that can happen to you, it can happen to your favourite actor on Grey's Anatomy, it can happen to your favourite musician — it can happen to anyone.

According to Psychology Today author Sherrie Bourg Carter Psy.D., "Burnout is a state of chronic stress that leads to physical and emotional exhaustion, cynicism and detachment and feelings of ineffectiveness and lack of accomplishment."

Stress is a biological response to challenging circumstances. This causes your body to release hormones, such as cortisol and adrenaline. Chronic stress is considered long-term stress and physically, the symptoms of stress won't subside.

Stress sucks. Chronic stress sucks. Burnout sucks. What's

even worse is that a lot of people don't know they are burning out until they are suffering. I'm sure that you've read a surplus of articles about burnout and have heard about different symptoms and negative impacts on your life.

Well, I'm here to reinforce that burnout is real. I'm not a medical professional, however, I'm as close to a certified workaholic as they get. Sometimes we are in positions where we must work as hard as possible in order to make ends meet. It might mean we fill all of our waking hours with work. This is what I had to do for many years and I was hooked on working. Guys, working this much isn't a good idea. Trust me.

ONE ISSUE IS THAT SOME OF US GET ADDICTED TO MONEY AND THE thrill of success, so we decide to fill all of our waking hours with work. Let me tell you, more work may equal more money, but it does not equal happiness.

This chapter isn't about an epiphany I had, but it's about how burnout can seep into your life and slowly take away who you truly are. Being self-employed, I once felt like I always had to prove something to someone. I didn't go to school to become a doctor or lawyer, so in order to make over six figures a year I thought I needed to hustle hard and work harder. When I first started off as a business owner, I had to put a lot of hours in that didn't directly convert to money, but instead growing my reputation and building relationships.

But as my business grew, all of those hours I put in came back in the form of clients who hired me. I guess you can say I am addicted to the thrill of landing a new client. I love the feeling the surges through me when I client agrees to work with me, and that is something that hasn't changed since day one of me making my first sale as an Avon lady.

I wasn't addicted to the money. I'm not addicted to money. I am addicted to the adrenaline rush that comes with bringing on new clients and achieving career wins. One issue I often ran into was an inability to say no when I was at my capacity. I felt guilty turning away work and was worried that if I said no that the work would dry up.

WHILE BUILDING MY BUSINESS, I HAD A FEW FRIENDS WHO WENT through burnout. While they were going through a very difficult time, I saw a lot of their symptoms in myself. Besides feeling like I wasn't able to hold on to the rapidly spinning Earth, the symptoms that I noticed were telling me to slow down and rest.

My eyes would twitch uncontrollably. I would try and hold my finger over my eyelid in hopes that it would stop. I felt like something out of an Alfred Hitchcock story. Was I slowly turning into a monster? The answer is yes, I was. I was a work monster.

I had no short-term memory. I couldn't remember everything that was being told to me without writing it down. My regular dose of anxiety was rapidly increasing to an uncontrollable feeling and my heart felt like it was going to beat out of my chest. The Prozac that I take for my Pre-menstrual Dysphoric Disorder (PMDD) didn't seem to help.

My fuse was short and the littlest things would set me off. People chewing loudly and high pitched beeps did not stand a chance in my presence (but really, I just complained under my breath or to my husband). You could almost see steam coming out of my ears.

I was exhausted. I couldn't seem to feel rested, no matter how much sleep I got. It was hard for me to generate creative ideas, which is something I'm great at. My brain felt empty. I wanted to be a hermit, which was rare because I'm a very social extrovert. I am an ENFJ, after all.

I knew I was tired. I knew I was burning the candle at both

ends, but I had goals to achieve and tasks to accomplish. However, these goals didn't even matter to me anymore because I felt empty. After a while, some of these symptoms felt normal and became a part of me. I wore these symptoms as a badge of honour. After all, I felt like this because I was moving mountains with my company. I felt like I couldn't take time off - even if I had a warm beach vacation planned, I would still bring a little bit of work with me.

I've heard stories of people's bodies shutting down from stress. I've heard of people having to take leaves from work because of stress. I've heard of people making huge career shifts due to burnout. But, why did they let it get so bad? Was it because of societal pressure?

Eventually, I knew I had to make a change when I stopped caring about the projects that I was working on. My passion was gone.

I never let stress get to the stage of hospitalization or needing medically prescribed time off, but it was close. A few years ago, right before my husband and I were to leave for our European rock n' roll honeymoon, my plate overflowed and I hit my limit of clients (a limit that I didn't think existed). I committed to a big project and it took up a lot of my mental bandwidth and time that was allotted to other clients. This meant that I had to fill my Blair-time with work, which was a boundary that I blurred. Before long I was working from the moment I opened my eyes until I crawled into bed, plus weekends. I wasn't able to rest my brain and I was operating at full speed. I felt like I was on fire, but really, I was burning out.

After much thought I decided that I was going to let a few longstanding, easy to work with, well-paying clients go. It was a hard decision that I question now, but it's what I had to do at the time. I was making a career pivot and I no longer could take everything on. As I bid farewell to many thousands of dollars per month, I hopped on a plane for our honeymoon, my first vacation without a laptop or iPad in over a decade, and completely checked out of work.

I actually came home feeling refreshed, which was a sensation that I hadn't felt in years. Imagine coming home after a vacation and actually feeling relaxed. What a concept!

Over the next while, as life happened all around me, I did what I needed to do to ensure that I was taking care of my mental health and protecting myself from chronic stress and burnout. A few things that I do to protect myself from burning out are setting boundaries and expectations of when I'm available; ensuring that I start each day with going for a walk in nature, to yoga or to the gym; and making sure to say no to things that don't fit on my plate, which is a challenging practice.

My flame represents my passion, my soul and my life and I now I try to aggressively protect it. I'm aware of how I'm feeling and I do what I can to protect my mental health and creativity. Don't forget to closely guard your flame because the world needs you to keep shining bright.

Key Takeaways:

1. Know the signs and symptoms of burnout so you can catch it before it fully engulfs you.

2. Set boundaries and make sure that you create space and time in your schedule that is not used to work.

3. Stress is really bad for both your physical and mental health, so explore different ways for you to manage stress.

15
THE YEAR OF ABUNDANCE

"What you believe, you receive."

- Gabrielle Bernstein

IN THE BOOK *THE UNIVERSE HAS YOUR BACK: TRANSFORM FEAR TO FAITH*, Gabrielle Bernstein shared the following truth bomb: "Universal Lesson: We are not responsible for what our eyes are seeing. We are responsible for how we perceive what we are seeing."

We have various ways to look at each situation. How we perceive it and create the path to achieving a certain goal can be in our power. I'm only human and sometimes I forget this, but when I'm in alignment with this notion, I'm able to attract what I want into my life.

I truly believe in the power of manifestation. I always knew that manifestation was legitimate, but my recent binge on all things related to Gabby Bernstein (social media, books, blog posts and beyond) has strengthened my belief. For those of you who aren't sure of what the word 'manifestation' actually means, let me explain:

Gabby defines manifesting as "cultivating the experience of what it is that you want to feel — and then living and believing in that experience so that you can allow it to come into form."

To me, this definition is the perfect explanation. If you are new to the concept, you may want to learn the basics on how to manifest. This chapter focuses on one of my personal manifestation experiences. I highly encourage you to do your research on manifestation and try it out for yourself. It's very powerful and has changed my life in more ways than I can count. I guess you can say I've been manifesting well before I realized that I was doing it.

Back in the coupon company ownership days, I was going through things in my personal life. So, my mom and I would start each day by texting uplifting sayings back and forth to one another.

I wanted to give that gift to the world so I worked with my website developer to create a tool that shared a new positive message every day. This tool was available on my website and I offered it as a free tool for others to embed on their websites.

That's right, folks: I created a free embeddable widget that I called the Daily Emotional Forecast. Sadly, that tool no longer exists, but every now and then I think about reviving it.

Although I believe that manifestation is always present, my awareness of it comes and goes. It was only recently that I started diving deep into Gabrielle Bernstein's work and was reminded about the power of manifestation. This allowed me to reflect. While I was processing her content and thinking about what I want to do with my life, I had a major life event occur.

LET'S REWIND TO THE BEGINNING OF 2019, WHEN I SET GOALS AND

chose a word to represent my year. What I didn't do was be specific about the intention for that word and the universe definitely gave me a couple of very big assignments.

The word I chose was RESILIENT. At the end of 2018 our family learned that my father's chronic pulmonary obstructive disorder was in the end stages and, without a lung transplant, he only had a few years or less to live.

This completely threw me into a vortex of darkness, especially because we've only been getting to know each other over the past decade. In my 20s I forgave my father for being absent in my life and began to build a relationship with him. It has been a beautiful and challenging experience. You see, my whole childhood all I wanted was to have my father back in my life and now that he is back in my life, he is being taken away from me.

In December 2018, I lived life in a fog. I wouldn't drink to escape my problems, but if I had a drink, my problems seem to disappear. Due to anxiety, I could not function during the day and my mental and physical health were suffering. I was getting weird cuts that would not heal and caught a bizarre stomach flu, which is something I don't usually get.

I KNEW I HAD TO MAKE SOME BIG CHANGES IN MY LIFE. I DECIDED that as of January 1, 2019, alcohol would no longer be a part of my life. Eventually clean eating followed that choice and now I do my best to maintain self-care. I regularly go to the gym and yoga, get my nails done, go for massages, go to an acupuncturist, and other various things that help me maintain my physical and mental health.

In January 2019, when I selected my word to be "Resilient", I didn't include any other information in my workbook or out loud or to the universe. I was not clear about my intentions for that word. From that moment on, the universe began to show me how resilient I really am.

In the spring of 2019, I attended a workshop that helped change the way I saw my situation. The workshop was for entrepreneurs and focused on being more soulful. We did a few exercises and what we worked on shed a light on some of my goals that I didn't even know existed. A few days later, on a Monday morning, I woke up feeling energized with the idea for the I Am Resilient Project. This idea literally dropped into my mind and wouldn't leave. I felt empowered and just knew that I had to ride this wave.

AFTER PUBLICLY SHARING MY STORY OF FORGIVENESS AND THE news of my dad's health, a shift happened. People began to share with me that my story empowered them to forgive someone or make a positive change in their lives. WHOA (imagine this being said in Joey Russo's voice)!

The I Am Resilient Project was created to be a community where people can share and read stories of resilience. It can be cathartic and healing to share your story. It can be inspiring and motivational to listen and learn about other people's journeys.

One can often feel alone while navigating a challenging time and my hopes for this community were that people wouldn't feel alone and they would know that they had our love and support. Everyone deserves to tell their story and that is why I created this community.

As I began to build the I Am Resilient Project, I continued to manifest my resilience. The second half of 2019 was challenging. Shayne and I had multiple expensive truck issues that impacted our ability to go camping (which is what I live for).

. . .

My Zaida Jack, who was like a parent to me, passed away on my husband's birthday. We had to immediately fly home because funerals in the Jewish religion happen right away, which led to more expenses. On our way home from the funeral trip, we got in a car accident on the highway, which resulted in me suffering from whiplash and a concussion. While trying to recover from my concussion, I launched a product for one of the brands I work with, which meant no time to heal. Finally, this fall, when I was starting to heal, my husband suffered a minor heart attack and had quadruple bypass surgery. I survived all of those things because I am resilient.

When life gets hard you have to take things moment by moment and day by day. I persevered in each of those situations and did what I had to do to survive them.

I decided to admit to the universe that I understood how resilient I was and that I was ready to manifest and welcome a new word into my life.

The I Am Resilient Project is the beautiful rainbow that came after the shitstorm that 2019 was. Sometimes you have to survive the hard times in order to grow. 2019 inspired me to choose the word "Abundance" for 2020. I'm welcoming in an abundance of happiness, an abundance of good health, an abundance of career success and an abundance of money.

As I wrap up this chapter, I'm currently participating in Gabby's 21 Day Manifesting Challenge. I'm manifesting a few very exciting things, including international speaking engagements and a healthy pregnancy.

With my mission to share my story and knowledge, I know that I'll reach my speaking goal this year and 2020 will be the year that baby Blair is created.

Key Takeaways:

1. Manifesting is real and anyone can harness the power of manifestation.

2. When manifesting, be clear and detailed with what you are manifesting and your intentions.

3. "In the midst of the darkness, grab a flashlight." — Gabrielle Bernstein

16

FLEX YOUR RESILIENCE MUSCLE

"Do not judge me by my success, judge me by how many times I fell down and got back up again."

- Nelson Mandela

WE ALL DO VARIOUS THINGS IN OUR LIVES TO STRENGTHEN WEAK muscles or body parts. We do this as a preventative measure so that we are strong and prepared for the unknown. We do this when recovering from something, or even when trying to achieve a specific goal. However, not all "muscles" exist physically. Our society needs to begin to working on strengthening our resilience muscles.

A lot of us begin to strengthen our resilience muscles at a young age. Resilience is the ability to bounce back from a difficult time. We, as humans, are built to be resilient. Let's be honest, if we weren't, we would crumble and not survive.

When I was a child, I was not taught about resilience or given strategic tools to strengthen it, but due to various challenges in my life, I built this muscle up on my own. I believe every challenge in life is preparing me for the next stage of my life.

The first time I remember being resilient was when my parents divorced when I was eight years old. My family, as I knew it, was going to change and so would various aspects of my life such as family dinners and who I was going to live with. At the time, I was unaware that my father was living with addiction. This prevented him from being the father that I deserved. I was now going to live with my mother and younger sister, while only seeing my father sporadically and of his own accord.

As a child, I didn't know about his mental illness, so I simply thought that my father didn't love me anymore. However, later in life I did learn that he does love me, but he was unable to show it because of his addiction.

Our mother did everything in her power to keep the lives of my sister and I as similar to our peers and community as possible. We were now living on a single income with no financial support from my father. Our mother worked as much as she could, received bursaries, funding and support from our extended family, along with help from friends, to ensure that she was giving us the best life possible. She was still able to provide us with a good education (including Hebrew school, the University of Winnipeg Collegiate and university), sent us to summer camp, registered us for lessons (swimming, dance and beyond) and put food on the table. Our mother is the picture of resilience and having her as my role model helped me to build up my resilience.

WHILE GOING THROUGH THIS MASSIVE LIFE TRANSITION AS A child, a few other things helped build up my resilience. I used creative outlets like writing poetry by candlelight, spent time with friends and family, spoke with the school guidance counselor, and was kept in a routine by our mom. Society knows a lot more about mental health these days than we did back then. I think it would have been beneficial for me to have been told, in a way that I could have understood, that my father was sick. This may have helped me understand his absence in my life. I also wish that I began seeing a therapist a lot earlier in life.

These days, to help protect and manage my mental health, which positively impacts my ability to be resilient, I follow rules that I've set for myself. I no longer drink alcohol and at the time of writing this chapter I've been without it for over a year. I also start off each day with movement, ensure that I eat to fuel my body, get at least seven hours of sleep a night and take breaks when I'm tired and need to rest.

I MAKE TIME TO DO WHAT I'M PASSIONATE ABOUT — I SPEND A lot of time in nature and go camping whenever I can. At 9:00pm, every day, my gratitude alarm goes off and I share three things that I'm grateful for from the past 24 hours, which I have been doing for over four years. I also have a therapist and am open about my struggles and journey with the tribe of people I surround myself with. I'm not perfect and I still have bad days, but recovering from those days seems to be getting easier and easier.

Doing all of these things helps to build my resilience. I'm able to be resilient in both my personal life and my business life. I plan to always be strengthening my resilience muscle. 2019 was a challenging year. It aged my soul, but I was able to navigate each challenge. It was hard, but I was able to do it with the unconditional love of my husband, family and friends.

You have probably been strengthening your resilience muscle your entire life without knowing it. Now that you are aware you have that ability, I recommend that you add some new elements to your resilience-strengthening regime. Prepare yourself for what's to come while making your light shine brighter.

My recent challenges inspired me to build the I Am Resilient Project - a community to inspire people to navigate and overcome their challenges. This community was built for you and can be found at www.iamresilient.info. Here you can read and submit stories, sign up for our newsletter and learn about events and community initiatives. I've already begun to work on my next book, which will be stories of resilience from around the globe. I can't wait to bring that book to life. I am resilient and so are you.

Key Takeaways:

1. Prioritize your mental health and do what you can to take care of you first. You cannot pour from an empty cup.

2. Practice gratitude every single day. It's a gift to find at least three things from your day that you are grateful for.

3. You do not need to suffer in silence and you are not alone.

4. You are resilient.

17
THIS IS ONLY THE BEGINNING

"Destruction leads to a very rough road,
but it also breeds creation."

- Red Hot Chili Peppers

BEING AN ENTREPRENEUR IS A BEAUTIFUL THING, BUT IT'S HARD AS eff. You have an endless amount of opportunities. You are in control of your life and future. I'm honoured that you chose to allocate your precious time to reading my book. By the time you are reading this final chapter, I'm sure the ideas are floating around in your head, ready to be implemented.

As my company, Blair Kaplan Communications Inc., approaches its business Bat Mitzvah and becomes a woman (AKA it turns twelve this summer), I've had time to reflect. I'm always learning new lessons and reaching new milestones.

There are no right or wrong ways to be an entrepreneur and most of the time it won't happen overnight. Keep putting one foot in front of the other and do what you need to do to work towards your goals.

There are many different aspects to being a business owner - it all starts with your heart, passion and desire. If you feel pulled to starting your own company and taking control of your career, follow that feeling. It won't be easy in the beginning, but it will get easy. It will be a lot of work, yet you will feel extremely liberated. If I can do it at the age of 23, I have faith that you can pull it off too, and make it happen.

Take the leap, be fearless and make sure you know who you are and what you stand for. Your magnetic passion will draw people to you, like a moth to a flame. If you lead with your heart, put the hours in to grow your company, spend time networking and support your community, good things will happen to you and your business.

Every opportunity and experience that you have is setting you up for whatever is about to come next. The moments you feel like you failed are when you begin to build something different and beautiful. Those unavoidable feelings of defeat will happen and those are the times when you truly push yourself to your creative limit. After the storm comes the rainbow and destruction will breed creation.

BEING AN ENTREPRENEUR REQUIRES RESILIENCE, PROFESSIONAL development, a willingness to be open and vulnerable, and finding comfort in the discomfort brought on by growth. If you are looking for ongoing support, it's out there. I'm out there. Actually, I'm right here (unless you are reading this while on the porcelain throne - then I'm waiting for you in the next room). Now that you have been given some key lessons to help guide you, go apply them.

Don't keep your passion, side hustle, new business, growing

business or goals a secret. Scream it from the rooftops, tell the world, rip off the band-aid and start your business!

Spread your wings and take the leap. Feel that entrepreneurial drive pulsing through your veins because it's what will help you soar high.

ACKNOWLEDGMENTS

Writing a book is 110% not an easy task. I had very specific writing goals and milestones that got derailed numerous times, but that is okay because I still accomplished my goal. With the support of my community, I achieved a dream that I've had since I was a little girl and successfully published my first book. To all of the humans who have been a part of my entrepreneurial journey and supported me along the way, thank you.

The biggest shout out and gold stars go to my mother and sister. Mom, you have always supported my ventures, encouraged me to pursue my crazy ideas and will forever be my number one fan. Alana, your wit and encouragement is something that I'll be eternally grateful for. The completion of this project would not have been possible without the support and help from both of you so thank you from the bottom, top and middle of my heart. I love you both a googolplex.

My book would not have come together as well as it did without the support of my business coach and book-writing mentor, Mike Skrypnek, the Founder of Grow Get Give

Coaching and author of Entrepreneurial Secrets to Grow Get Give Life. Thank you for believing in me and my goals and for keeping me accountable. I'm excited to see where this journey takes us.

Over eight years ago I was given a gift from the heavens and it was my in-laws, Valerie and Dave Venables. I'm incredibly lucky that they are so supportive and cheer me on in everything I do.

Although my current relationship with my dad is still fresh, I'm grateful for all of the knowledge and support he provides. His resilience and strength are admirable and I'm honoured to have his entrepreneurial drive. Dad, thank you for the daily morning messages. I love starting my day with you.

My writing was put on pause when Shayne had a heart attack. The day of his open heart surgery I spent five hours alone. I didn't speak to anyone during that time and I felt calm and at ease. I never really felt alone; I just knew that everything was going to be okay. While waiting for Shayne to be transported from surgery to the CSICU, I met another lady who was waiting for her husband to come out of surgery. I learned that they were rushed to St. Paul's Hospital from out of town. She seemed worried and stressed out. I spoke with her and helped calm her nerves. After talking for a while, I asked her name, and she said it was Zaida.

Only a few months prior I lost my Zaida Jack – this was a gift, a sign from him that everything was going to be okay. I knew he was with me the entire day. My grandparents, Zaida Jack, Baba Leah and Baba Ruthie were a very important part of my life. They spent a lot of time with me, nurtured my creativity, and encouraged all of my passions. My Baba Leah is still alive and I know how proud she is of me. Baba, thank you for everything that you have done for me.

Gabby Bernstein, your knowledge and energy helped me

navigate my husband's heart attack, surgery and recovery. I was guided to you by the universe and will be forever grateful for your content, especially your audiobooks.

Husband, Vnab8or, Shayne, thank you. You love me unconditionally at my worst (stress, depression, anxiety) and even more when I'm at my best. This book brought out some pretty intense emotions in me and you always remained positive and supportive. I'm lucky to have you by my side in life and I'm so grateful that you and your new heart helped to see me through this book until the end.

This book is for all of you out there who can't and won't settle for a standard 9 to 5 job. Your ambition and lack of conformity is admiral and always remember, especially in difficult times, YOU GOT THIS!

ABOUT THE AUTHOR

Blair Kaplan Venables is an expert in social media marketing and the president of Blair Kaplan Communications, a British Columbia-based PR agency.

As a pioneer in the industry, she brings more than a decade of experience to her clients, which include global wellness, entertainment and lifestyle brands. Blair has helped her customers grow their followers into the tens of thousands in just one month, win integrative marketing awards and more.

She has spoken on national stages and her expertise has been featured in media outlets including CBC Radio and Thrive Global. Blair is the author of Pulsing Through My Veins: Raw and Real Stories from an Entrepreneur and is already working on her second book. When she's not working on the board for her local chamber of commerce, you can find Blair growing the "I Am Resilient Project," an online community where users share their stories of overcoming life's most difficult moments.

SHARE THIS BOOK

Share **Pulsing Through My Veins:** Raw and Real Stories From an Entrepreneur with the entrepreneurs and future entrepreneurs of your life. To place an order call 604-838-4234 or email blair@blairkaplan.ca

Retail: $14.95 USD

5-20 books:
$12.95 USD each

21-99 books:
$10.95 USD each

100-499 books:
$8.95 USD each

Hire Blair

Blair Kaplan Venables is the edutaining speaker that you need at your next event! To book Blair to speak, M.C., lead a workshop, facilitate a panel discussion or give a keynote:

Blair Kaplan Venables
Blair Kaplan Communications Inc.

604-838-4234
blair@blairkaplan.ca
www.blairkaplan.ca

NOTES

NOTES

NOTES

NOTES

NOTES

NOTES

Copyright © 2020 by Blair Kaplan Venables

Editing by Sarah Rose Sinclair

Formatted for Print & E-Book by runandjumpbooks.com

Cover Design by whistlercreative.ca

All rights reserved.

No part of this book may be reproduced in any form or by any electronic or mechanical means, including information storage and retrieval systems, without written permission from the author, except for the use of brief quotations in a book review.

Manufactured by Amazon.ca
Bolton, ON